PARENTING A SCORPIO KID

Understanding A Scorpio Kid.

Lance.K.Andrews

Contents

INTRODUCTION

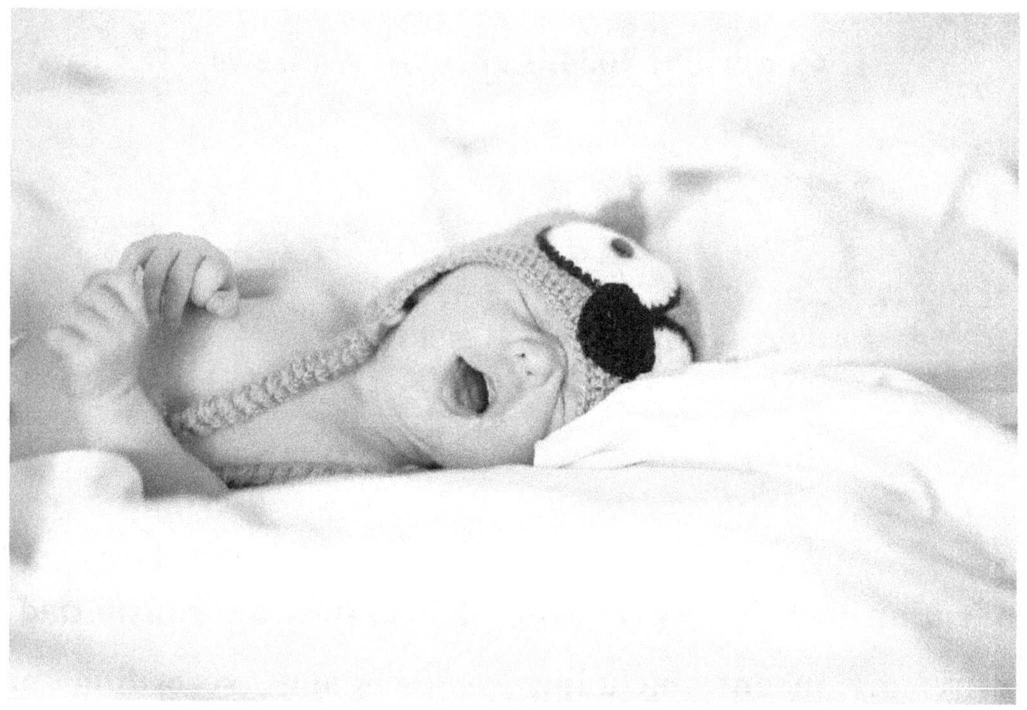

Dear Parent,

Welcome aboard the journey of raising a Scorpio child! It's truly an honor to have you here, and I want to express my heartfelt appreciation to you for choosing this guide.

As a parenting counselor, I've witnessed the transformative power of understanding and embracing the unique qualities of each child, especially Scorpios. Your decision to invest in this book shows your commitment to being the best parent you can be, and that is something to be celebrated.

I wholeheartedly believe that good parenting is the cornerstone of a better society. By taking responsibility and learning how to navigate the ups and downs of parenting, we can prevent many of the challenges and traumas that children face.

Together, let's embark on this journey of discovery. In these pages, we'll delve into the intricacies of your Scorpio child's personality and provide practical strategies for handling both the good and tough times.

Thank you for trusting me to guide you on this path. I wish you all the best as you navigate the joys and challenges of parenting a Scorpio child.

With warm regards,
Lance

FACTS & METAPHYSICAL ASSOCIATIONS

Dates: October 23- November 22

Symbol: The Scorpion

Key Phrase: "I Desire"

Planet: Pluto (Mars)

Birthstone: Opal (October); Citrine (November)

Number Vibration Numerology: 9

Element: Water

Flower: Chrysanthemum & Rhododendron

Color: Deep red

Day: Tuesday

Chakra: Sacral/Naval Chakra (Svadhisthana)

Chinese Zodiac Twin: Boar/Pig

Funny Chinese Zodiac Twin: Boar/Pig

Tarot Card Association: Death (Scorpio), The Tower (Mars)

Healing Crystals: Amber, Aquamarine, Bloodstone, Jasper, Malachite, Ruby

Celebrity Scorpios: Grace Slick is a mega Scorpio with 5 – count them five – planets in Scorpio. Others are Shere Hite, Ti-Grace Atkinson, Sally Field, Leonardo DiCaprio, Charles Prince of Wales and Pablo Picasso

SCORPIO SYMBOL AND ITS MEANING

Every spring when Orion sets, Scorpio rises as a reminder of its poisonous bite.

Sailors considered this sign of the Zodiac as a negative Omen. Egyptians recognized this pattern as a sacred serpent, and alchemists felt that the time of Scorpio (fall and winter) was the best time for their golden endeavors.

The Greek story goes that Orion went to Crete on a hunting expedition with Artemis. He brazenly said he would kill every creature, making Gaia downright pissed.

She sent the Scorpion to sting him for his conceit. Artemis, Leto, and Zeus intervened to have Orion put in the sky but not without the Scorpion as a constant reminder that you don't mess with Mother Nature.

A Scorpio's every thought, every word, and every deed is tied with Golden Threads to the pursuit and capture of love.

It doesn't matter the form but giving and receiving love at its purest, highest, and most divine vibration is the only thing that gets a Scorpio out of the proverbial bed in the morning…

Hold…wait for it…else they would stay there all day. ●

Oh, and BTW, Scorpios have a propensity for turning the macabre into a yuk yuk with one flick of their stinger.

Scorpios are creatures of evolution – ever-changing and growing as they mature.

There is no question the Scorpio personality has a dangerous side, but only people arrogant enough to think they can cross them without consequences have anything to fear from that sting.

Those a Scorpio loves barely even notice the potential risk, besides all that mystery is hard, if not impossible to resist.

Scorpios are incredibly strong people, not in the physical sense – rather they have a core made of steel. This is why they confront difficult situations and leave people reeling.

Do not get between a Scorpio and their current quest.
Really. I mean it!

Remember that the Scorpion is ruled by Pluto with all its magic and power. Pluto also gives Scorpios a profound 2nd sense – they know when they're being played and when you're keeping it real.

We might have forgotten to mention one little thing…

Like their twin soul Pisces, Scorpios give a whole new meaning to the word 'psychic'.

WHAT CAN I EXPECT FROM A SCORPIO CHILD?

Rules and authority

From a young age, tiny Scorpio can exert serious will, making their influence known. As the zodiac sign of power, little Scorpios are keenly aware of "who's who" on the metaphorical chess board and will strategically position themselves to curry favor with the key decision maker.

This systematic sign likes to know where everyone stands, particularly about them. If they could map out an "org chart" they would—grabbing the title of Executive Vice President of Children's Affairs, perhaps. Caution: ruling with an iron fist or being overly permissive can lead to a power struggle, as Scorpio doesn't trust anyone they perceive as either weak or domineering.

Limits

Limits might make this security-seeking sign feel protected because Scorpios detest being uncontrollable. Their probability of an unpleasant surprise is reduced when they know what to expect, like burning themselves on a hot stove or scratching themselves on the cat's tail. Oh my! Naturally, a lot of Scorpios have to learn the hard way. Scorpio may give you the classic fierce Scorpio glare while looking you in the eye and willfully disrespect you. This child's mantra is **"I dare you to stop me."** When that occurs, you have to set very hard boundaries since a Scorpio won't stop pushing the envelope.

Separation and independence

Scorpio is the sign of bonding and has a strong need to be attached—often through physical closeness—to the (slim) few people this little one trusts. Heading back to work or dropping off Scorpio at daycare? Not so fast. Scorpio could have some powerful emotional outbursts when you first leave their side. You may need a transition period while slow-to-trust Scorpio warms up to a secondary caregiver.

Younger siblings

Scorpio is the sign of jealousy and possessiveness. One day, the little sibling may be "mine!" Other times, Scorpio may get a touch of the green-eyed monster, especially if they feel displaced or one-upped by a scene-stealing sib. Should this happen, Scorpio will maneuver things—or act out—to regain his stronghold.

Older siblings

Because Scorpios enjoy being pampered, they will gladly take in their siblings' attention. Putting all of that aside, Scorpio doesn't want to be regarded as a helpless, flighty little child. Despite being a head shorter than everyone else, this sign wants a respectable place at the big kids' table! When an older sibling makes fun of Scorpio, they will immediately become defensive and even competitive. Because cutting Scorpio is skilled at striking back when it matters most, verbal combat can be vicious.

Ouch!

Bye-bye, baby: Weaning, potty training

Since Scorpio is the sign of connecting, it can be difficult for this attachment-driven sign to wean. Little Scorpio is averse to parting with anything that offers safety and comfort. If potty training is presented to Scorpio as a calm, methodical procedure, it can be rather simple. But if it turns into a power struggle or they feel like they have to make a fast change, Scorpio will back down. This sign enjoys having control over everything, including when and how they use the restroom!

Learning: School, homework, and teachers

Scorpio's powers of concentration are unrivaled, and this observant kid can be a sharp little student. This sign may have one or two subjects that they pour all their energy into since they like to focus. Because Scorpios can have such great memories, they often do well on tests and quizzes and can be early talkers. They're also competitive and will want to be the strongest, fastest, and smartest kid in class.

Household conflict

Private Scorpios don't want to be involved in the messy venting of emotions that don't concern them. They'll withdraw into their little haven, blocking out the outside world and losing themselves in a book or television program. Naturally, Scorpio is frequently the cause of strife in the first place, particularly if they have siblings. Scorpios are a fighting breed. If a sibling enters Scorpio's territory without authorization, there can be a severe reaction!

PERSONALITY TRAITS OF A SCORPIO CHILD

The sun sign, Scorpio, comes from the large constellation of the Zodiac, **Scorpius**. The constellation was identified in the second century by Claudius Ptolemy. And, over the centuries, has been an important part of Astrology as the eighth sign of the Zodiac.

A Scorpio is someone who is born between **October 22** and **November 21.** If your little one's birthday falls in this bracket, you have a Scorpio baby. Would you like to know what a Scorpio child is all about? For starters, they are the ones who don't hesitate to enter the unknown. Let's get to know some more Scorpio baby personality traits!

Here are some Scorpio Zodiac traits you may see in your Scorpio baby:

They are leaders

Your Scorpio baby might already display signs of fierce independence. Scorpio kids tend to enjoy taking charge. This quality, in turn, will help her develop leadership skills if honed correctly.

They pay close attention to details.

Yes, Scorpio children are meticulous in their approach and pay close attention to detail. That's one reason why you've been noticing your Scorpio baby's coloring books look neat over time, which brings us to the next trait.

They are perfectionists.

Your Scorpio child will tend to get it right sooner than you expect.Their ability to pay close attention to details makes her the perfectionist she is. Neat notebooks, properly arranged toys, sometimes color-coordinated dressing, etc. are just a few examples of what your Scorpio child could use this trait for.

They like freedom and privacy.

Scorpio children like to do things their way and are a little sensitive when it comes to their privacy. If your child has been ferociously stubborn about doing something, you know where it's coming from.

They like the unexpected.

As mentioned earlier, Scorpios do not fear the unknown. They enjoy an unexpected dish, an unexpected journey, an unexpected gift, etc.; they are ready to take on whatever comes their way.

They are picky about friends.

Now, this might raise concerns, but not to a great extent if you teach your child to be kind and respectful. However, your Scorpio baby is more likely to have only a few friends because they are quite particular when it comes to letting someone into her inner circle.

They are honest But It's difficult to win their trust.

Scorpios are known to be honest, brutal sometimes. There is a chance you could find yourself in a tricky spot when your Scorpio child blurts the truth in the middle of you handling a situation sensitively. In other words, diplomacy doesn't go well with Scorpios. they do not trust others easily; therefore, some people could need to put in extra effort to win their trust and never lose it again.

Memories make an important part of their lives.

Scorpio babies never let their memories die because they cherish them so much. Sometimes you could be surprised when your Scorpio youngster remembers something you had completely forgotten. For this reason, a Scorpio will never forget any emotional or previous pain.

They are pensive.

One of the traits that set Scorpio babies apart is that they like musing over things. Their train of thought is constantly running, and they might need some diversion to relax a bit.

They're intense!

Children who are Scorpios tend to be very intense and have tremendous emotions. They are ferocious and capable of equal amounts of love and hate. They never use half-measures when acting! They either put out their best effort or none at all. They are naturally competitive and might be challenging to manage as a result.

They're intelligent

Scorpio kids are highly intelligent. They have a keen mind, which shows through their singularity of purpose and commitment to a task. This intelligence is displayed very early on, and many Scorpio children tend to stand out in class.

They yearn for meaningful relationships

Scorpio babies have strong emotional bonds with those who are close to them and provide care, especially. They must be treated with respect, whether that means having candid discussions or being as open and honest as you can. Open communication and thought-sharing are encouraged.

They can be secretive

Secrecy is one of the traits associated with the sign of Scorpio. Scorpios have a propensity to isolate themselves and hold their emotions and ideas inside. You must instill in them the value of communication from an early age as a parent. They value having a close relationship with a loved one, and if they feel comfortable confiding in you, they will open up to you about their deepest feelings.

They're moody but wilful

Scorpios are known to be moody. When something's not going right for them, they tend to brood and their mood can change at the drop of a hat. They are also very sensitive to vibes, which means they're attuned to the feelings of their loved ones. You can't hide a lot from your little Scorpio!

Being ready to deal with a strong will is necessary when raising a Scorpio child. They will make an effort to obtain what they know they want. You must impose discipline on them softly and with firmness while still showing them love. Might and force won't go you very far. They will just become more obstinate.

They are determined.

A strong sense of determination characterizes Scorpio's children. Once they set their sights on a goal, they exhibit unwavering persistence to achieve it.

They are very curious

Scorpios have a natural curiosity that drives them to explore the mysteries of life. They ask probing questions and have a keen interest in understanding the depths of various subjects.

SCORPIO CHILD

Scorpion Girls

Scorpion girls apply the game philosophy of 'hide and seek' to communications. Until a parent reveals a part of him/herself, these children remain silent. Telling these little girls a secret makes them feel trusted.

Scorpio thrives on the darkness, so these girls are often curious night owls. Keep in mind, the mysterious allure of these girls will attract boys easily.

Scorpio girls have high sensitivity levels and an outlet to release emotions will help them immensely during their teen years. Also, these girls have a strong drive to attain the tools to support their future goals.

Scorpion Boys

Scorpion boys have strength, good health & a fair amount of aggressiveness that needs taming in their childhood. Parents of these boys need to consistently stress the need to respect authority & even, to loose gracefully. Once finding the right balance with structure and affection, a Scorpion boy will respond to his parents with honesty and frankness.

Scorpion boys, especially teen boys, have a strong need to retreat to their space/bedroom when processing stimuli or big life events.

Scorpion boys seek truth and expect promises to be kept. As teens, these boys will need modeling on how to be sexually responsible & to respect girls.

The ever-alluring Scorpio has a very resilient look about them. They tend to have well-defined features and shoulders that defy Atlas in terms of their ability to carry problems. Two of the most sensuous areas are the Scorpio lips and neckline. They have average heights but still manage to shine in a crowd.

Scorpios like to dress well, but not necessarily to grab attention (remember that secretive nature). They have a good immune system but may experience various accidents because they take risks, particularly in their youth.

In terms of eating, the Scorpio likes good food and they need it for energy. You rarely find a Vegan in this lot who could well live the saying **"protein is us"**. Once they hit midlife, many born under this star sign put on weight but they wear it well.

Having a Scorpio Child is a bit like having a beautiful onion with layers and layers… and yet more layers. Plus, they are likely to cause others to shed a tear or two… or a hundred.

There is so much going on inside the Scorpio child that others are never allowed a glimpse of. It is simply (as the saying goes) **"a Scorpio thing."**

First, this fiery star sign has a spooky knack for reading people accurately. Scorpios are the most psychic of all the 12 zodiac signs. If you're not certain of the truth, see how your child responds to a person or situation and watch their Spidey Senses in action.

Scorpio kids are so clairvoyant that when he/she tells you they were just talking to great granny (who died before they were born) pay attention. They are likely not making it up.

A child born under this zodiac sign is incredibly smart (genius runs rampant with this lot) and adoring, but they also have a greedy and sometimes down-right scary spiteful side.

Their reactions to, well, everything, can prove quite surprising/shocking and create chaos wherever they are.

However, this is because emotions run extraordinarily deep with Water Signs. Whereas others can let things 'roll off their back', the Scorpio Child feels every single word and deed in the farthest reaches of their soul.

Knowing that every Scorpio has intense emotional highs and lows, which are amplified tenfold throughout childhood, can be very beneficial.

Put on your life jacket first and ride the waves with your Scorpio child to best assist them in navigating the maelstroms they have created for themselves. Scorpio kids are therefore uncontrollable since they lack fear. Unconditional affection elicits the best response from Scorpio youngsters.

Recall that Mars is the also ruling planet of Scorpios, therefore even the youngest Scorpions will resist criticism and throw down the gauntlets. Your home will be far less dramatic if, when it comes time to be tough, you do so out of love rather than domination.

A Scorpio's forgiveness of any transgression is difficult, whether they are an adult or a child. Compared to adults whose life experiences have somewhat tempered their tails, Scorpio youngsters are more likely to demand retribution.

After a disagreement, they would far sooner walk away from a lifelong friend than attempt to work things out.

With these kids, it's all or nothing, therefore you have to be quite consistent with your upbringing (the Scorpio child is skilled at finding ways around things).

A Scorpio's parent must always be truthful, never telling a small white lie, since they take a long time to trust even their closest friends and family. The traditional **"Do as I say"** mentality would never sit well with the Scorpio youngster.

Engage your child in conversation at a level that corresponds to their intelligence by being involved and hands-on. Hugs and other expressions of affection are welcomed by the Scorpio child since they are beneficial to them. They become more safe within the family and have more self-confidence as a result.

But keep in mind that Scorpios are not as talkative as certain other signs. Until they feel ready to share, a lot of what they think and feel might stay a secret.

Having said that, the Scorpio sign is most recognized for its sex drive (don't shoot the messenger). More than any other sign, the Scorpio youngster is likely to be lured to sexual exploration at a young age. In this, and given their natural proclivity for secrecy, working to keep the lines of communication open as regards intimacy can help keep your ***preteen, tween, or teen*** safer than they might be if left entirely to their own devices and, uh, vices.

It's probably time for that second drink, huh?

These children have amazing control over their emotions and an intensity that makes you feel like you're seeing an adult in a child's body. They have passion, intense insights, a great need for security, and the ability to bounce back from nearly anything.

SCORPIO GIRL

The Scorpio Girl is very profound and intense. She has an innate beauty and unique personality that truly sets her apart from others.

Get used to her wanting privacy. This girl only shares some things with a select few people, if at all. She will prick everyone who tries to break through her enigmatic exterior. Because of their need for independence, your daughter will constantly ask you to explain your stance, and you can experience some power conflicts, particularly during your *adolescent years*.

Girls who are Scorpios are very driven and future-oriented. What career path does your daughter wish to pursue? She will always be drawn to the resources that will help her do that.

Oh, certainly, that aim may change with age, but the determination remains and rewires itself for the next great quest.

Generally speaking, your daughter will prefer to keep things private. It may make direct conversation challenging. To gain a glimpse into someone's thoughts and soul, you may have to expose some parts of yourself. They will adore games like *hide and seek* where they have to hide objects with the same determination! And confide in a Scorpio if you ever want a secret kept. It satisfies their demand for secrecy and gives them a sense of trust.

Your Scorpio daughter might turn up to be a bit of a night owl. That entails setting up a nightly schedule for her that promotes good sleep hygiene. It won't be simple to do this. Because they think all kinds of things are waiting for them in the dark, Scorpios thrive there. As they grow, this explorative nature turns into questioning. These will not be the simple parental questions either.

Hint: if you honestly don't know an answer, say so but then find out a factual answer for them later, otherwise their imagination will run amok.

A Scorpio child's level of sensitivity has no bounds. Your daughter can hold on to upsetting memories because she doesn't want other people to witness her happy tears. Make every effort to assist her in letting go of such feelings, especially as they get older. By the way, Dad, grab your shotgun; your daughter's allure will draw in **potential suitors** due to her mystique. Even strong parents find it difficult to resist the Scorpio sign's charm, so be ready to put in extra effort to see past your daughter's surface-level flirting.

SCORPIO BOY

Generally speaking, your Scorpio Boy will be quiet until they reveal something. Similar to the females in the species, they frequently long for independence far too soon.

The Scorpio Boy will probably enjoy numbers in school and may concentrate on a career in finance. These guys like to be in charge, whether it's at school or home, so you have to constantly remind them who is actually in charge.

Male Scorpios enjoy taking charge in the household. This child has to have his aggression subsided before he gets his first black eye, but he is strong and healthy otherwise. The male Scorpio youngster needs to learn from his parents to respect authority figures and how to be a decent loser. It takes a great deal of continuous consistency for both of these qualities from mom and dad, but helps the Scorpio throughout their life, not just childhood bumps.

Scorpios are Water-natured, therefore parents must strike a balance between being severe and continuing to exhibit affection. The Scorpio retreats even deeper into his shell in the absence of that. In contrast, the Scorpio lad usually reacts with candor and forthrightness when bestowed with consistent rules and copious amounts of affection.

Boy, Scorpios have a strong sense of territory, especially those in their teens. He will retire to his room when he needs time to reflect and make sense of the world. Never enter that sanctuary without permission or without regard for what it stands for. The Scorpio can escape from excessive input in this "cave" (sensory overload is unpleasant for them).

Scorpio boys have some traits in common with girls. They want the truth and expect promises kept. Unless you have a very good reason for breaking your "code" with your son – stick to it like glue. As young men, they're as attractive to others as the Scorpio girl and should receive some grass-roots talks about sexual responsibility so that companions don't turn into trophies.

Ashley King, A parent of a Scorpio says:

"Oooooooo. A Scorpio son. May I get you a glass of wine? Maybe a double-shot margarita? LOL ●

Yes. I have tons of advice for you because I'm a Scorpio and I was a handful as a child. OK. Still am. But…. LOL

The first thing I can tell you is never, ever say, "No". Now, I'm not saying to give in all the time – far from it! But a Scorpio's mantra is "I desire" and its ruling planet is Mars. So, when someone tells a Scorpio 'no', they see it as an invitation to war!

It's much easier to redirect your 3-year-old's attention than it is to engage in a battle of wills.

Also, what's even harder to understand about a Scorpio is this:

Scorpios want one thing and one thing only – true, everlasting, and unconditional love and loyalty. So, when a parent gets into a "war" with their Scorpio child it sets up a no-win situation for the parent. Scorpio will fight 'to the death' for something they want – even if that means going to war with their parent. But their parents are who they most want to love them! So, fighting makes a Scorpio fearful that the parent will love them a little less and that just causes a whole other issue.

The bottom line, with Scorpios, redirection is the key. That and constant reassurance of how much you love them.

Finally, it would help to know your own Zodiac Sign. That way, you can take a look at how best you can communicate and interact."

Scorpio Kids And Maturity

Scorpio children have one of the hardest paths toward maturity. They have a dense web of emotions to discover, grow through, and master. A lot of parents give up on their Scorpio children or don't give them the attention that they deserve. Parents will cut their Scorpio kids short, which in turn can give the children mental complexes.

Scorpio children have a challenging path to face. They are the first sign in the zodiac to encounter and recognize death. This can be very overwhelming, as you can imagine. Some parents distance themselves from their Scorpio children because they think they're weird. This is one of the worst things you can do to them. Don't let your child feel like they're a misfit in the family or unwelcome. They need to be included and invited. **(A vampire won't enter your house unless you invite them, by the way.)**

A CHALLENGING SCORPIO CHILD

Scorpio children can be a handful. They're independent, aloof, emotional, expressive, attached to their families, and pretty strange. Scorpios need attentive parents who can embrace the full scope of their child's emotions since Scorpio children want to explore some very deep topics. They're ambitious, and they can be trouble-makers.

- **Rebellious**: Scorpio children are often rebels. They like to do things their way. They question boundaries.

- **Emotional**: Your child may have outbursts, anger issues, depression, or anxiety. They need reassuring parents who give direction and not too much discipline. Your support of them matters.

- **Complex**: Your child may like the villains in movies rather than the heroes.
- **Contradictory**: They may seem mature for their age and at other times amazingly immature. They might do extremely well in school or poorly.
- **Creative**: They'll likely make interesting clothing choices in high school.
- **Watchful**: Scorpio is constantly observing people.
- **Sensitive**: They're in tune with the vibes that people and settings give off. They prefer a grounded, nourishing home over one with too much discipline.
- **Ambitious**: They have a deep desire to be successful.

Scorpios are born in autumn, and this gives them an interest in disguises and transitions, like from season to season or from life to death.

As a parent, understanding astrology can help you better understand your child. All Scorpios have certain things in common with their Sun sign. Studying the Scorpio sign can help you cater your parenting style to your child or teen's personality.

Don't panic if your child is a Scorpio and you don't have a lot of experience with this sign. Scorpios may seem scary, but honestly, they're some of the best children you can have. They'll love you back deeply if you meet their needs, and you can count on them to make sure you're well taken care of when you reach old age.

Scorpio Is a Fixed Sign

The fixed water sign is Scorpio. This indicates that your youngster is obstinate and has a distinct taste in things. Scorpios are fierce advocates of their beliefs. Even if their chosen course causes confusion or offense to others, they will follow it nonetheless.

The Scorpio is intensely passionate, tenacious, and occasionally disciplined because of the fixed energy. Scorpios' fixed modality makes them prone to self-criticism. Although your child will always try to be the best at anything, occasionally their aspirations may cause them to become blind.

Fixed personalities make decisions. They are not readily persuaded to change their minds. They prefer things to be firmly established, with strategies in place. Scorpio kids could take offense if you frequently alter your plans or if you never make plans that fit their interests. It hurts their feelings when you are fickle. They want you to love them and never sway from that.

Scorpio's Season Is Fall

Fall, when the Scorpio child is born, is dominated by Halloween and other fall-related events. Compared to other children, your youngster might discuss and think about death a lot more. They have thought of dying. Most of the time, they're not attempting to scare you, but they are aware that everything is fleeting. They want to live their life to the fullest and be as passionate as they can since they know that nothing lasts forever; otherwise, they feel exhausted and find it difficult to accomplish anything because of despair.

Your child may be intrigued by costumes and disguises. They may seem to wear a metaphorical mask and try to hide from you. They're very private and will expect that you give them privacy. They sometimes feel more comfortable expressing themselves as an actor, in disguise, in a costume, or with a flashy outfit.

Scorpio children sometimes put on displays as a way to protect themselves—the disguise is their armor. Don't make a fuss over their acts; just accept them. If you accept their armor, in a way, you accept them.

Your child may seem sweet and sour. They'll likely want to give you love but also want to mess with you. Think of them as trying out different expressions to gain emotional understanding and charisma. Your Scorpio child will likely go back and forth on giving you treats and tricking you.

Many Scorpio kids like wearing darker clothing, such as *rich purples, blues, and blacks*. They don't feel that everyone can see them, thus they don't necessarily want to wear bright colors. Since many Scorpio kids are very conscious of their appearance, they could expect you to give them more attention than your other kids do when it comes to fashion and hygiene. There is a hint of materialism in Scorpios.

If you are the parent of a Scorpio child, you should put more of an emphasis on nurturing them than on trying to outdo them. A youngster born under the sign of Scorpio may be addicted to competition, therefore they may fall for your bait. Parents who are competitive need to be cautious about how they agitate their Scorpio child. Be careful to instruct them on how to behave well as sportsmen. With the right parents, a Scorpio can be a powerful force of empathy. Scorpio children often prefer their moms, since women often let themselves be more nurturing. Scorpios will gravitate to parents who:

- **offer them more hugs and reassurance,**

- **cook them good meals,**

- **help them with chores,**

- **have self-control,**

- **are not too hard on them, and**

- **are slow to anger and quick to love.**

Don't fall for a Scorpio tantrum trap. They're trying to get the worst out of you and get you to show your crazy side. Instead, calmly guide them out of tantrums—you'll win their respect this way. Scorpios are very sensitive, so if you're mean to them or discipline them too hard, they'll take that to heart.

This child may push your patience, so you may have to slow down to think things through so you don't amplify the situation or turn it into chaos. It may seem like a simple singular moment, but what you do as a parent is lasting. **You make up part of your child's inner voice as an adult.**

22 INSIGHTS THIS DAD (MR. ADAMS PHILLIP) LEARNED ABOUT SCORPIOS BY RAISING ONE

"My adventure in understanding Scorpios began the day my daughter, Kenna, was born on **11/11/2020**.

Right from the start, Kenna brought a whirlwind of emotions that I hadn't quite experienced with my other children. It became clear to my wife and me that this parenting journey would be unlike any other.

As the months went by, my wife and I noticed something special about raising Kenna. She brought an intense emotional energy that permeated our home, unlike anything we'd felt before. We had to adjust not just to the external changes that come with welcoming a new member into the family but also to a profound transformation within ourselves. It was like a journey of discovering more about ourselves and how we could understand and support Kenna, who had this amazing power to see things others might miss. This ongoing involution within our family became the starting point for me to learn more about what makes Scorpios unique, using Kenna as my guide.

One day, while In our living room, I and my wife created a makeshift fort to keep Kenna safely within boundaries. Little did we know that she possessed an innate ability to discover vulnerabilities and exploit them! With no training or previous exposure to such situations, Kenna effortlessly pierced through our fort's defenses. Witness this extraordinary moment, captured by my wife on her iPhone.

Observing Kenna's remarkable discovery left me awestruck. In response, I turned to my Angelic Guides and asked Them to show me all the unique gifts that Kenna, and all Scorpios, inherently possess. From that moment on, I began observing the small, everyday details of Kenna's life, noting each revelation along the way.

1. **"No" is not in a Scorpio's vocabulary.** "Impossible" and "no" might as well be words from another universe. If you tell a Scorpio that something

can't be done, they might nod and say, "Okay," but behind that seemingly agreeable facade, they're already plotting how to prove you wrong — which, as sure as the Sun shines, they will certainly do.

Phrases like **"It can't work"** or **"That can't happen"** hold no power over a Scorpio; they're null and void. All a Scorpio needs to hear is, "Let's make it happen" or "I'll figure it out." But be prepared because they will scrutinize your work for pressure points and vulnerabilities. It's as if they have Divine knowledge straight from the Heavens. So, it's wise to get things right on the first try, but don't fret if you don't. Scorpios are here to reveal the weaknesses that often escape our notice. Your role is to recognize and fix them.

2. **Scorpios will push boundaries relentlessly**. The previous point is so vital that I'm emphasizing it once more, but from a slightly different angle. Scorpios will not entertain your excuses or limitations, yet here's the paradox: they'll push the boundaries of both.

To coexist harmoniously, you must excel at what you do and constantly push your limits. If you make a habit of testing your boundaries daily, you'll find it much easier to stand your ground when answering a Scorpio's questions, causing you to grow and expand in every area of your life.

3. **Scorpios can see everything you hide.** They possess an uncanny superpower to detect and reflect hidden vulnerabilities. This includes objects, systems, as well as the aspects of yourself that you'd rather keep concealed.

They'll mirror these vulnerabilities back to you, catching you off guard at times. They do this so that you are aware they can perceive, sense, and understand your hidden aspects. It's important to remember that it's not a personal attack; it's just a fundamental part of who they are.

From what I've observed, they apply this skill in interactions with both humans and animals, but I have yet to witness how it extends to the mineral and plant kingdoms.

4. Scorpios love to hide sh*t. To us, it might seem like they're hiding stuff for no apparent reason. However, trust that everything they do is methodical and well-planned. They are masters at the art of hiding sh*t, and if we can't discern the reason behind it, it's likely because they don't want us to know. I have yet to understand why they do this. But hey, perhaps they reserve some secrets exclusively for themselves.

5. **When a Scorpio likes something, they're all in**. You might discover yourself listening to one of their favorite songs on an endless loop until they decide they've had enough. Their loyalty is unwavering once you've earned their trust. However, it's crucial not to jeopardize that trust, as losing it can lead to them cutting ties with you.

6. **Make no mistake; Scorpios are the boss, and you are not.** When a Scorpio is ready for your opinion, they will give it to you. Scorpios possess a

clear vision of what they want to achieve and who they've chosen to accomplish each task. And when the final symphony comes together, keep in mind that it's the conductor who receives the credit. To collaborate successfully with them, you must set aside your ego.

(Gerald, A Scorpio kid)

7. **Scorpios are also known for their unwavering determination and commitment to their goals**. They have high standards for the people they associate with, and expect excellence from those around them, whether it's in personal relationships, work, or any other aspect of life. They appreciate competence, reliability, and excellence in others because surrounding themselves with capable individuals helps them achieve their objectives more effectively.

8. **Scorpios place a high value on routine and organization.** Scorpios thrive when they have a structured daily schedule and a sense of order in their

lives. Though their lives may resemble chaos to you, know it is excessively organized to them, which is all that matters.

9. **Scorpios have a unique ability to find joy and appreciation in life's simplest pleasures.** While they may be known for their intense and passionate nature, Scorpios also have a deep appreciation for the little things that often go unnoticed by others such as attention to detail, living in the present moment, and connection to nature.

10. Occasionally, **Scorpios may feel the need to retreat to a private space** and have a good cry. This might seem sudden or random to others, but it's an important part of their emotional processing. During these moments, they are not necessarily sad or upset; instead, it's a way for them to release pent-up emotions, gain mental clarity, and reset their emotional state.

11. **Scorpios are here to experience the extreme ends of 2 polarities**. Scorpios are ruled by Mars and Pluto, two powerful planets symbolizing both life and death (transformation). These celestial influences drive Scorpios to explore the extreme ends of whatever captures their attention. Sometimes, they may deliberately break or destroy things they care about, not out of malice but to understand and explore the consequences fully. Finding a harmonious balance between creation and transformation remains a continuous journey for them.

You mustn't attempt to interfere with this process. They are safe to experiment in this way, as their observations will lead them on a journey of involution.

12.. **Under no circumstances shall you cross a Scorpio**. They will go from zero to fifty-thousand in 3 seconds. You do not want to experience their "sting." You've been warned.

13. Scorpios, being influenced by two ruling planets, thrive on having **choices**. They must always have options available. Even if one choice is better or the second option seems like nonsense, it's crucial to present them with multiple choices — one of which better be your best.

14. **You cannot imprison a Scorpio**. Their confinement is always of their choosing, driven by a desire to experience something unique. But rest assured, when they decide it's time to break free, Cosmic Law dictates that a clear and easily accessible exit appears before them. Even if you lock a Scorpio in the deepest, darkest pit in the center of the earth and seal it with concrete, when they decide they've had enough, the Universe will conjure a doorway from the very heart of existence, offering a safe passage to their chosen destination. See the video at the beginning of this article for an example.

15. **When Scorpios feel it's time to move on, let them go.** Scorpios naturally seek shifts in polarity, a change in the energy around them. If they

haven't mastered articulating or communicating this desire for change, it might show up as you feeling frustrated around them. This is a sign that it's time for a change of environment or for you to leave. It's not a personal judgment on you, it's part of their cosmic rhythm. You may re-enter their presence when they are ready for you.

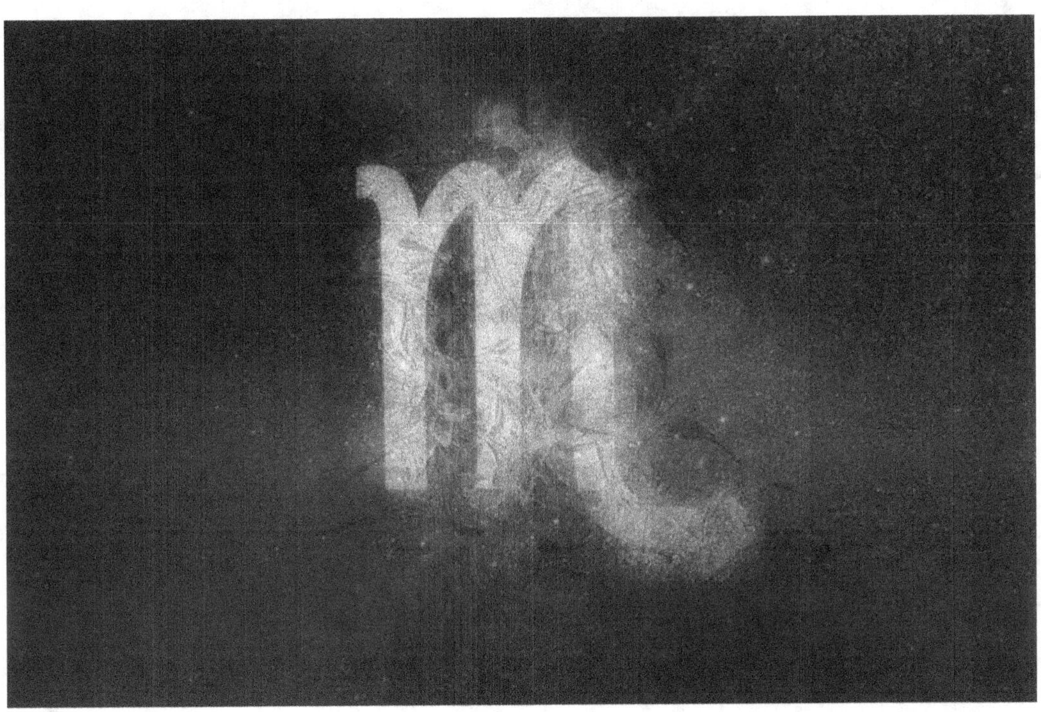

16. **Scorpios have no boundaries when it comes to spaces.** Your area, your workspace, even your most private spaces like the bathroom, or your moments of deep thought and meditation — nothing is off-limits to them once they decide to explore it. You'll have to accept this, as it's an inherent part of their nature, and there's no changing it.

17. **Scorpios need to wake up on their terms,** exactly when they're ready, and not a moment sooner. Their schedule for waking up is entirely their own,

and it can change at their whim. If you attempt to rouse a Scorpio before they're prepared, be prepared for the consequences, as it may take hours (or an entire day) for them to rebalance. Consider yourself warned!

18. **Scorpios have the power to do anything they desire** as long as they can come up with or create a reason for it. This reason can be the most insignificant thing imaginable; it doesn't matter — and frankly, their reasoning is irrelevant. They just need a reason, then the Universe will support their actions because they are destined to explore any direction they set their focus or attention towards.

19. **Learn to embrace your sh*t because Scorpios see sh*t**. They'll notice your sh*t, and as long as you're comfortable with them seeing your sh*t, it will be overlooked. However, if you show discomfort or resistance to your sh*t being seen, they won't hesitate to point it out, often quite boldly, which might trigger you. Instead of getting upset, use that moment to learn how not to judge your sh*t. Laugh it off.

Over time, as this situation repeats itself, you won't be triggered by your sh*t anymore. You'll become less sensitive to their observations, and these moments will have served their purpose, which is your personal growth. Let the record show that you can avoid all of this sh*t, by learning to be ok with your sh*t, which was stated at the beginning of this point.

20. When you're not watching, **Scorpios will often try out all the things** you've specifically told them not to do. Trust that they sit patiently and wait until the Universe tells them *"Now is the time to try our little experiment."* To manage this behavior, it's best not to outright forbid them, except when it involves their safety. Instead, find ways to allow them to experiment within certain boundaries, pushing the limits while ensuring they remain safe.

This experimentation is essential for them to develop their skills in testing the vulnerabilities of systems, something they are naturally inclined to do. Your role in this process is to strike a balance between what's considered *"safe"* and what's not, which may require you to confront and overcome your fears. Remember, Scorpios are also evolving through this process, and it serves a purpose in their growth.

Happy child

21. **Scorpios benefit greatly from expanding their vocabulary.** As my daughter continues to grow and express herself using more words, forming 2

and 3-word sentences, I've noticed that her emotional frustrations have lessened. Many of her outbursts stem from her struggle to convey her feelings or intentions. Over time, as we continue teaching her new words, I anticipate her frustration will further decrease.

When Kenna is upset due to communication challenges and I can't immediately discern her needs, I employ a simple yet effective approach — I ask her to "show me." This usually helps me understand what she's trying to convey at the moment. I can already see that by expanding her vocabulary and helping her express herself better, she experiences fewer emotional frustrations. Until then, we view these intense moments as opportunities for both her and us to learn valuable lessons from the Universe.

22. **Scorpios want what they want when they want it**. If you give them what they want, all will be well in your world. Don't, and they will vocalize their displeasure with you in a very Scorpio way. You've been warned.

I acknowledge Kenna's other astrological placements that contribute to her character. I also acknowledge that not every Scorpio will display all of these traits, but many might share some of these qualities. Keeping these observations in mind should help you connect better with Scorpios.

My adventure of raising a Scorpio child has been truly extraordinary, and I encourage you to explore your unique gifts and those around you. Know that each sign contributes something special to our world.

I hope you've enjoyed reading my insights on Scorpios. To wrap things up, I'd like to share an aphorism my wife often tells our daughter Kenna:

"It's oooohhh-kaaay. Everything is going to be oooohh-kaay. Just breathe."

I believe this can benefit us all."

THE THREE DEVELOPING STAGES OF SCORPIOS

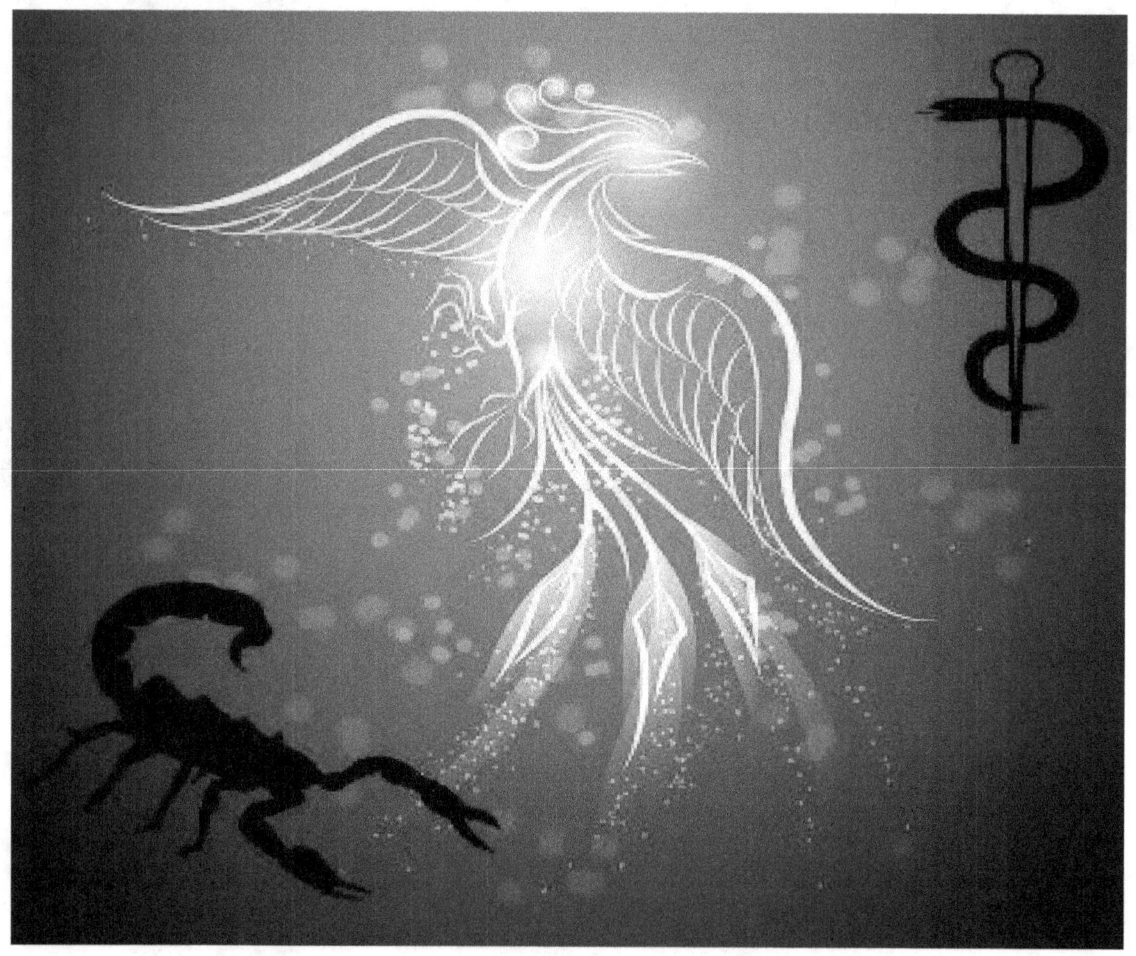

Scorpio children have one of the hardest paths toward maturity. They have a dense web of emotions to discover, grow through, and master. A lot of parents give up on their Scorpio children or don't give them the attention that they deserve. Parents will cut their Scorpio kids short, which in turn can give the children mental complexes.

Scorpio children have a challenging path to face. They are the first sign in the zodiac to encounter and recognize death. This can be very overwhelming, as you can imagine. Some parents distance themselves from their Scorpio children because they think they're weird. This is one of the worst things you can do to them. Don't let your child feel like they're a misfit in the family or unwelcome. They need to be included and invited. (A vampire won't enter your house unless you invite them, by the way.)

Scorpio is symbolized by the **snake, the scorpion, and the phoenix**.

Scorpio children have so many emotional expressions, which are reflected in the sign's symbols. Most of the Sun signs only have one symbol, but Scorpio has the most symbols attached to it with three:

1. Snake

2. Scorpion

3. Phoenix

The Scorpio will have to go through these three stages in its development. Parents, you might not see your child in their final phoenix stage, since this often isn't reached until adulthood—and even later adulthood.

Stage 1: The Snake - Scorpio starts as the snake. It slithers around like a predator, looking for ways to survive. The snake is cunning, brash, sneaky, and manipulative. The snake stage isn't very caring or kind. It's more about getting what it wants when it wants, and making sure its plans go accordingly.

The snake is very protective of its kind; it prefers the night, and it wants things cool and not too hot. The snake may keep to itself and only reveal its heart to those it trusts.

How Parents Can Help With This Stage

Getting your Scorpio youngster to trust you will be crucial. They might abruptly cut you off. If they do, don't freak out, but be mindful of their limits. You can push them more away if you complain that they have shut you out.

Stage 2: The Scorpion

Eventually, the snake will morph into the scorpion, which isn't a great place, either. The scorpion is essentially the snake but with legs and poison. The scorpion is deadly, it moves quickly, and it also can be pretty mean to those that it loves.

How Parents Can Help With This Stage

During this phase, your Scorpio child aspires to shine, make an impression, acquire authority, and conquer the world. It makes sense to provide them with a variety of sports and other competitive activities in addition to voluntary work.

Scorpio receives a great deal of male energy from Mars in addition to a great deal of yin and feminine energy from Scorpio. As a parent, you must assist them in striking a balance between these things so they can grow up and operate as a whole.

A youngster that has a lot of Mars energy has to be active to release it, and they also need a parent who can help them control their hostility.

A child with a lot of yin needs a very reassuring environment—they need a parent who can direct them through their sensitive ways.

Scorpio kids might do well to have their garden that they can nurture. This is helpful both for aggressive and sensitive kids.

Stage 3: The Phoenix

The phoenix is a challenging stage to master. Often, Scorpios will briefly enter the phoenix stage and then cycle back to the snake and scorpion. It takes practice to master the phoenix stage and stay in it for long periods.

The phoenix is all about sacrifice. They care about others and know that, to overcome existential crises, one must follow the golden rule: Do to others as you would have done to you.

How Parents Can Help With This Stage

Kids aren't often recognized for their selfless actions. The Scorpio must be given opportunities to make sacrifices, demonstrate their compassion for others, and even put others' needs ahead of their own if you want them to grow up.

The most important thing parents can teach their Scorpio child is this: **Survival is not as crucial as sacrifice**. Don't expect them to ace this course in one sitting; it will take a lifetime. Scorpio is fascinated with development, phases, and levels; with the correct conditions, it will evolve from the snake and scorpion. Scorpio is a symbol of progress and the mysteries of maturity.

HOW TO STUDY THE WATER ELEMENT IN TAROT

In Tarot, the water element is symbolized by the house of cups. The cups from Ace to King go on a path through emotional development. With a Scorpio, it will be key to follow their emotional development and help them grow into a kind, wise, and well-tempered adult.

Your child will likely go through dozens of moods as they mature from child to teen to adult. They'll need parents who can reassure them and give them direction, parents who are sensitive and kind, and parents who recognize them for their unique talents.

Understanding Scorpio via Tarot: Suit of Cups

Cards	Description	Meaning for Child
Ace of Cups	Indicates new beginnings	Your child may be drawn to new ideas, happiness, and relationships. They're drawn to success.

Two of Cups	Duality; two hearts or two minds coming together	Your child is drawn to having strong relationships with others. They are also courageous, loyal, and passionate.
Three of Cups	Dancing, friendship, merriment	Your child is drawn to activity and celebration. Scorpio children are known for their connection to Halloween.
Four of Cups	A young man sits under a tree and is contemplative.	A period of boredom and where nothing seems of interest. Your child may go through periods of inactivity where their emotions become distilled. They

		may need a moment to reset.
Five of Cups	Three cups are knocked to their side; two cups still stand.	Your child will have to confront disappointment or loss, and you'll need to direct them toward appreciating what they do have and the opportunities still before them.
Six of Cups	Two youths play in a garden surrounded by six cups.	Your child will hold onto memories and nostalgia.
Seven of Cups	A youth sees seven cups in the clouds with different fortunes and misfortunes.	Your child will encounter many different kinds of choices and must take

		the time to understand them. Your child has the power to take control of their emotions with the right guide.
Eight of Cups	Eight cups are arranged in a row. A figure leaves them behind.	Sometimes we have to go on journeys into the unknown. Your child will grow by going after new and unknown things. They can't always stay with what they know.
Nine of Cups	A well-fed, satisfied person sits with nine cups behind him.	Your child has the power to make their wishes come true. They should be careful about what they wish to happen.

Ten of Cups	A husband and wife join arms. A rainbow is over their house.	Your child is attuned to its family. Scorpios are some of the biggest relationship-seekers. Scorpio desires to be in a passionate relationship with a strong family.
Page of Cups	A youth holds a cup, and a fish pokes out of it.	Your child has insight and intuition. They would do well to study art, poetry, and music.
Knight of Cups	A knight offers a cup.	Sensitive, seeking, romantic, chivalrous
Queen of Cups	A woman sits on a throne.	She is intuitive and gives good advice.

King of Cups	A king holding a scepter floats on water.	Someone wise, tempered, balanced, and kind. This is the ultimate goal for Scorpio.

BEST GIFTS, PETS, HOBBIES AND PLAYTIME TIPS

Some Scorpios like the creepy crawlies like a **tarantula**.

Others are not so tuned to the proverbial dark side and look for a smart, persistent pet with a secretive allure. Try a **Burmese cat.**

If there are hobbies that combine the mind, body, and spirit the Scorpio will be even happier.

Wait until your Scorpio isn't expecting something then drop the surprise in their lap. Don't let your packaging give you away either. Suspense is delicious to a Scorpio!

Some items that suit the enigmatic Scorpio personality include **puzzles, treasure boxes, good mystery books, richly illustrated Tarot Decks, and scary movies.**

This water sign is especially talented in the arts or music. Start them young with toy instruments and craft sets and they'll entertain themselves for hours. The Scorpio child loves to compete, so enter them in contests where they can shine as individuals.

As the sign that rules transformation, many Scorpios love having an alter ego. Give them lots of dress-up clothes so they can go into costume. You may be shocked at how well they can emulate their favorite TV character or copy an accent. If you want to teach them a foreign language, they'll pick up on it quickly at a young age.

Scorpios are **fashionistas** and can be a bit fussy about playing games where they might get their outfits all dirty.

They'll prefer aquatic sports like *water skiing, surfing and boating*. Sign them up for swimming lessons early.

Highly intuitive, Scorpios are easily affected by other people's energy. Don't force them to play team sports or be a part of playgroups if they protest. They are particular and will make friends on their own.

Scorpios like having favorites: favorite toys, foods, friends, etc.

Learning their favorites is a good idea if you want to have an easy time keeping them occupied (**the babies can spend hours fixating on a musical mobile above their cribs**). Note: this sign can become obsessive, so you may need to nudge them to try new things.

- Choose playtime activities that stimulate their curiosity and intellect.
- Provide art supplies or open-ended toys to ignite their imaginative spark.
- Respect their need for independence and let them explore activities on their own.
- Plan outdoor activities that allow them to explore nature's mysteries.
- Use play to help them healthily express their deep emotions.

HOW TO DECORATE YOUR HOME FOR A CHILD WITH WATER ENERGY

I'm a big fan of decorating your home for your family's energy. If you have a Scorpio child, you may want to have a space for them that's based on the water element. Having a home that is open to their element can help them feel safe, accepted, and understood. They may not necessarily know that you are trying to build a home that fits their personality and needs, but they will feel the comfort it brings.

Indoor Ideas for Scorpios

- Try adding water fountains, snow globes, or water features into your home.

- Add more mirrors to your home. Water is about reflection, so mirrors can mimic that. Mirrors can help with the flow of energy. Your child might be a little vain, too, and would like to see their face from time to time.

- In Feng Shui, color is one of the easiest ways to bring energy into a room. To bring in a water feel, paint a wall blue.

- Add black and white pictures to your walls or watercolor paintings. Black-colored accessories offer a hint of the water element, and black gives a more masculine or yang feel to water energy. (Blue gives a more feminine or yin feel.)

- Add pictures of water landscapes to your home as well.

- Add in more furniture or other items with a blue color to help with the energy. Blue accessory pillows, rugs, towels, and window shades could also help to bring out water energy.
- Add antique blue glass in the kitchen and other places. Little signatures of blue can help you get the vibe you desire in your home.
- Water energy does well in the northern area of your home.
- Light fixtures could also help bring out that water vibe. Add in lamps that remind you of the ocean, figurines of mermaids, or lamps made of shells.
- Decorate with ships in bottles, navigational items, globes, and the like.
- Consider having a rain stick or rain noise in your home to help create the right vibe for your child. Water sounds can be soothing to them.
- Sharp and straight angles go with yang; curves go with yin. Water overall is more of a yin energy.

It's best not to add more water Feng Shui into a bathroom as it already has a lot of water features.

Outdoor Ideas for Scorpios

Children do well to go outside and learn from the elements. A Scorpio child will enjoy having a pond where they can watch fish, a creek that they can play in, a fountain they can enjoy, and/or a window or screened-in porch from which they can watch rain or snow.

- If you don't have an outdoor space or cannot incorporate water features into your yard, take Scorpio children out to rivers, lakes, or the beach to get some fresh air and watch the waves.

Animal Companions for Scorpios

In addition to other animal companions given before:

- Consider adding a fish bowl or aquarium. Scorpios will enjoy having pets: fish, lizards, and birds all go along with their journey's path.

- Scorpios also love cats and dogs. Scorpios sometimes shut out people, so it's a good idea to have a pet with whom they can feel more comfortable. Having a pet can also teach them responsibility and how to nurture something.

NURTURING HEALTHY HABITS

The water element rules the reproductive and lymphatic systems and body liquids including blood, mucus, and lymph. Water lubricates, flushes, and cools the body. Water signs are exceptionally sensitive to their environment, particularly to fungi, bacteria, and viruses.

Health issues for water signs generally have a strong emotional component. Water sign people easily pick up negativity from others. They tend to brood over their health and imagine problems to be greater than they are. Their health problems tend to recur in cycles.

Scorpio's cell salt is calcium sulfate, which is the prime ingredient in the repair of tissues and resistance to infectious diseases. The nose, mouth, throat, esophagus, reproductive organs, and intestinal pathways need this mineral for healthy functioning. A deficiency opens the way to colds and sinus infections that hang on forever, skin eruptions that do not heal, and infertility.

Eat: Foods rich in calcium sulfate, which Scorpios should include in their diet, are asparagus, cauliflower, radishes, onions, tomatoes, figs, black cherries, and coconuts. Scorpios need calcium food such as yogurt, and cottage cheese. They should concentrate on a diet high in protein, fresh fruits and vegetables & whole-grain breads. The following are particularly good for Scorpio: fish and seafood, green salads, beets, lentils, almonds, walnuts, citrus fruit, berries, apples, bananas, and pineapples.

Don't Eat: Scorpios should not eat large meals, and the evening meal should be light. Bottled spring water is often better for them to drink than regular tap water.

SCORPIO CAREER TRAITS

A Scorpio will work and work until they succeed, rarely admitting defeat. It is the challenge and accolade of succeeding at something deemed difficult that spurs a Scorpio on to professional success.

Being driven characters, Scorpios can clash with those they feel lack vision or motivation, and may become easily frustrated with colleagues who do not pull their weight.

Scorpios possess a thirst for knowledge and enjoy undertaking new challenges and learning new skills. They are well suited to analytical and detail-orientated tasks, particularly when these have the potential to make tangible improvements to the sector they have chosen to work within.

Although they enjoy working around problems, a wholly creative career may not be best suited to a Scorpio, since they tend to lean towards careers that appeal to their methodical and analytical traits.

10 Best Careers For Scorpios.

RESEARCHER

A career as a researcher is well suited to a Scorpio's practical and analytical mindset. Scorpios are meticulous when it comes to detail, so they will enjoy a career that involves carefully examining a problem or challenge, collecting sufficient data, conducting statistical analyses, and compiling, collating, and then clearly presenting the research so it can be published.

A setting where their research can be applied to make practical improvements, whether these be technical, medical, or social, will be fulfilling to a Scorpio.

As they like to be the best at what they do, Scorpios have the motivation needed to persevere and achieve the important breakthroughs needed in research.

ENGINEER

Scorpios make good engineers because it is a career that offers the opportunity to apply their analytical perspective to a practical setting. Engineers solve problems by analyzing systems and processes – ideal for inquisitive Scorpios.

Scorpios enjoy having a problem to solve, particularly if it provides an opportunity to use their comprehensive knowledge and display their skills. They are often best suited to the mathematical and methodical side of the role, excelling in considering and approaching challenges logically.

Scorpios enjoy having an impact, so working as an engineer and helping to create buildings, infrastructure or machinery allows a penchant for problem-solving to result in productive tangible outputs and improvements.

FINANCIAL ADVISOR

Scorpios are strong and strategic when it comes to handling and managing money. They are good long-term planners, carefully considering future impacts and guarding against potential issues.

They are, therefore, suited to roles like a financial advisor or accountant. They have an eye for detail and the stamina to sit and sort through financial records and data.

Scorpios like to achieve goals, and financial goals are no exception. They will gain satisfaction and a sense of achievement from helping others to identify and reach their financial goals, as they simultaneously seek to reach their own.

MARKET ANALYST

Market analysts use research to understand the drivers behind purchasing behavior and consumer choices. It is a career suited to a methodical mind, one that enjoys working out the reasons behind actions and translating these into valuable predictions.

Working as a market analyst involves being a problem solver for your clients, helping to predict behaviors and secure their success in the market. Scorpios enjoy the challenge of problem-solving to reach a goal and this is a career that enables them to do this.

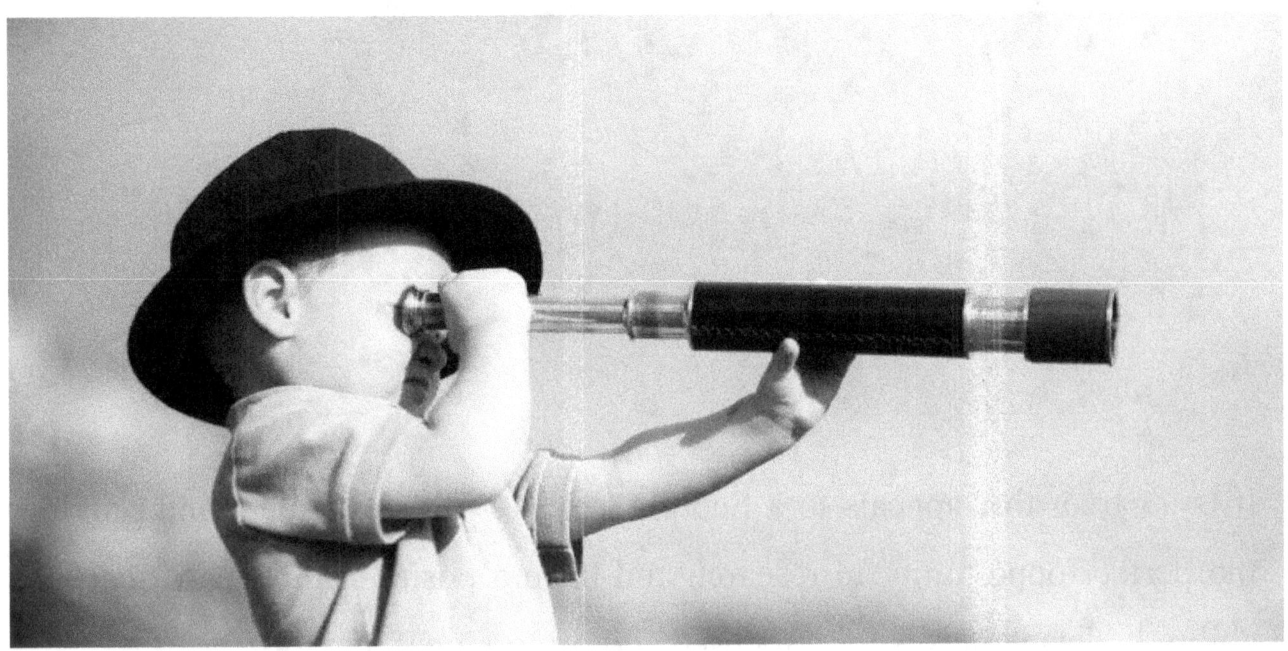

The role also provides a good balance of human contact and working independently. In this job, a Scorpio is still able to analyze people but will mainly focus on understanding their behavior trends from a distance.

PSYCHOLOGIST/PSYCHIATRIST

Scorpios make good psychologists or psychiatrists, as it is a career path that appeals to their curious, methodical, and problem-solving nature. They gain satisfaction from slowly piecing together clues from a patient's personal history, and assessing and exploring the potential impacts these may have had.

It is a career that appeals to a Scorpio's desire to investigate – and provides the perfect opportunity to research and have a positive impact. A Scorpio's ability to detach makes for a focused and professional therapist.

SURGEON/MEDICAL EXAMINER

Scorpios can detach from situations and perform tasks without letting their emotions enter into the equation. This is a useful quality when it comes to a career as a surgeon or a medical examiner. Being a surgeon requires a highly methodical and considered approach, as well as nerves of steel.

It is said that Scorpios protect themselves with an iron shield so that no one can affect them. They can withstand emotionally pressured or confronting situations that others would find difficult.

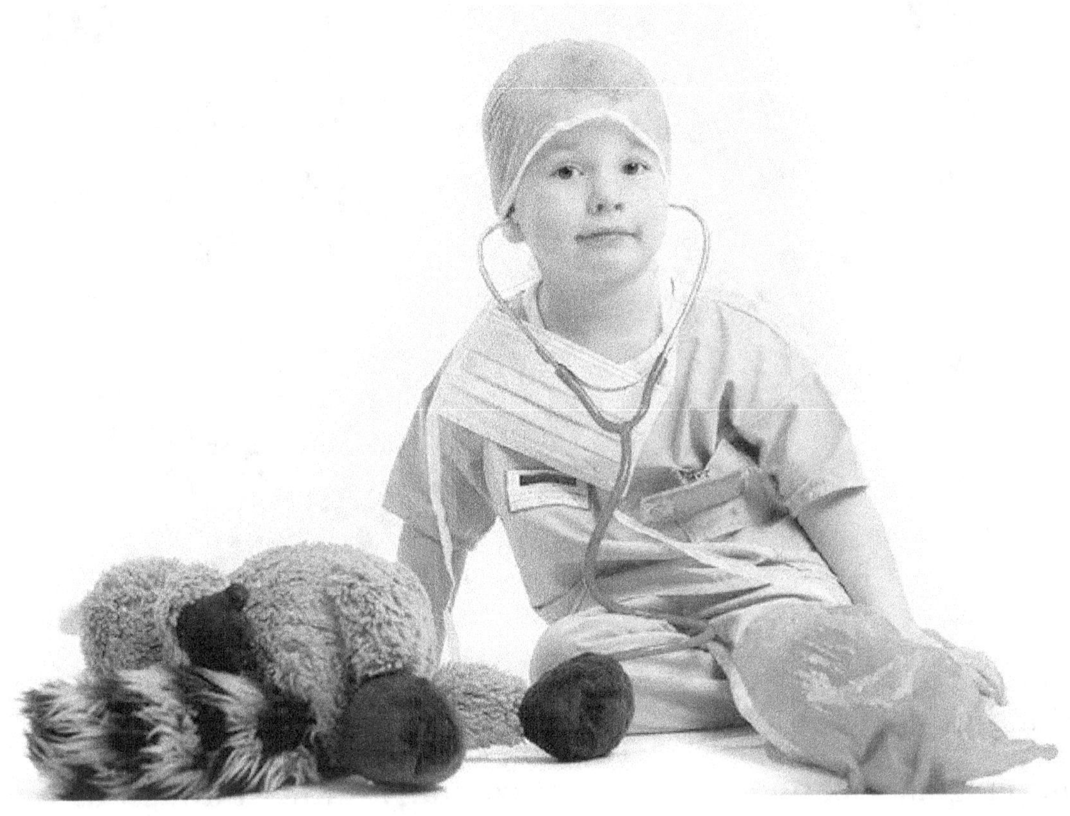

Working as a surgeon also taps into a Scorpio's need to succeed and achieve goals, making them dedicated and focused surgeons who seek to repeatedly excel in the operating theatre. They have an inner strength and drive that leads them to continue to persevere when it seems all may be lost.

While their need to succeed can be intense, Scorpios make the kind of driven, efficient, and meticulous surgeon you would want to be performing your triple heart bypass.

AUDITOR

Working as an auditor requires great attention to detail, coupled with a solid attention span. Scorpios are good at carefully sifting through data and have the stamina to see tasks that others may find dull through to completion.

Scorpios are adept at performing calculations and enjoy working with numbers. They are good with technical detail but also remember to look at the bigger picture. This means that while they are ambitious and focused, they are also balanced.

As they enjoy working independently and have a leaning towards careers that involve statistics, working as an auditor, accountant, or insurance broker will suit a Scorpio.

PHARMACIST

A career as a pharmacist offers a good balance for a Scorpio, providing some human contact but also the opportunity to spend ample time working alone.

It is a role that is scientific and well-regarded, requiring focus and attention to detail. These are traits at which Scorpios excels.

The communication part of the role of a pharmacist – making recommendations and ensuring patients know how to use their medications correctly – will appeal to Scorpios who enjoy the opportunity to blend their medical skills with their interpersonal ones.

CHEMIST

A career as a chemist or scientist is well suited to a Scorpio's scientific nature and love of analytical challenges. Again, it taps into their enjoyment of problem-solving and their drive to persevere and understand how things work.

For example, as a chemist, a Scorpio may be required to work out the particulars of a new reaction or explain unexpected chemical behavior.

Scorpios are committed and focused, able to endure and make the most of the hours of lab time needed to progress their work. They can be single-minded, which is of benefit when working on a niche and highly detailed challenge.

Work as a chemist is also fairly solitary, which can appeal to a Scorpio's focused and private nature, alongside their wish to make an individual impact or have a discovery attributed to their name. The feeling of controlling elements and reactions – being a **'master of the elements'**, appeals to the grand ambitions of a Scorpio.

DETECTIVE

This could be said to be the ideal career for a Scorpio, as it encapsulates all the skills and processes that a Scorpio most enjoys. Scorpios often enjoy or are well suited to other careers because of their detective-style elements.

A career as a detective appeals to a Scorpio's innate curiosity and desire to investigate and problem-solve. Scorpios make incredibly focused and driven detectives who fully commit themselves to resolving the cases they are given.

In this line of work, a Scorpio's ability to detach is also valuable as they may be exposed to emotionally confronting situations. Scorpios also tend to be skilled at quiet, discrete observation and have the dedication needed to gather all the facts required.

Being a detective also provides a Scorpio with the opportunity to be recognized for their achievements, whether through promotion, accolade or simply earning station respect for solving a difficult case. It is also thought that a Scorpio's penchant for revenge – perhaps more appropriately known in this context as justice – may drive them in this field.

Scorpios are meticulous and dedicated, their attention to detail and drive to succeed lead them to piece together events and solve crime cases with skill.

HOW TO PARENT A SCORPIO

Scorpios can be highly determined and curious children who may also require ample alone time to recharge.

Scorpio never does anything half-heartedly, and they pour their whole heart into whatever they are passionate about. If you have a Scorpio child, they may have an all-in or all-out approach to life. They may know exactly who they want to be friends with or what activities they want to do, and if something or someone isn't of interest to them they won't be afraid to let you know. Your Scorpio child also has a strong intuition, and they may be able to just sense when a situation feels off or one of their peers is upset. They're able to give helpful advice, and they tend to put on a brave face amid stressful situations. They want to understand how people work, and they may ask a lot of questions about specific subjects. Whether it's **dinosaurs**, **doctors**, or **arts** and **crafts** if your child is interested in a topic, they may get fixated on learning everything there is to know about it.

Give them some one-on-one time. Scorpios have a jealous streak, so if they feel ignored or think another sibling is being favored they are sure to act out. One caveat: these kids can be clever and cunning; don't get manipulated into favoring THEM!

Scorpios have incredible memories and will recall every slight fight from their childhood. Keep the home environment as calm and stable as possible to avoid spending a fortune on therapy when they are teens.

Reward them for sharing. The Scorpio child can be incredibly possessive at times, to the point where you might hear them saying "mine!" a little too often. As early as possible, teach them the power of paying it forward. Praise them each time they are generous with siblings and peers.

If You're a Fire Sign…

If you are an Aries, Leo, or Sagittarius parent to a Scorpio, you can teach your child how to release all of their strong emotions healthily. Your Scorpio may often have intense reactions or be super sensitive to what people tell them, so you could be good at showing them how to express their feelings rather than harboring grudges towards people. You also have a naturally optimistic and outgoing personality, while your child may be a bit more introverted. You may want to push them to sign up for after-school sports or plan monthly day trip adventures together to a local spot or a nearby city. You're able to encourage them to get out of the house and see more of the world. However, try to be mindful of your child's need for privacy and space from time to time. You can be pretty high-energy, but your Scorpio may not always feel the same.

In addition, your Scorpio child may put a lot of pressure on themselves to do everything perfectly, and they like to feel like they're in control in most areas of their life. You might be good at helping your child step back and take a look at the bigger picture, and you're able to show them the upside and the learning experience that comes out of every challenge.

Your Scorpio may need periodic alone time to recharge themselves. They might not love huge social outings, as they would rather hang out with the people closest to them, whom they can trust. While they may not have a big friend group, they are usually fiercely loyal to those they care about. The one area where your Scorpio child may face struggles is in learning not to control so much. They have a fierce determination, and they can get fixated on having situations go a certain way, but they have to work on trusting that everything happens for a reason.

If You're an Earth Sign...

If you are a Taurus, Virgo, or Capricorn parent to a Scorpio, you can be the rock that your child leans on when they're feeling emotional. You like to stick to your tried and true everyday routines, and your Scorpio child will appreciate the structure you provide for them. By following little rituals and having a set plan for their day, your Scorpio may feel more emotionally grounded and secure. In addition, you can teach your child how to practice **patience**. Whereas your Scorpio may make decisions quickly, based on their initial gut instincts, you tend to have a slower, more level-headed approach to planning out your life. You can show your Scorpio how to think things over instead of immediately saying no or strongly reacting to anything they don't like.

Because your child can get a bit fixated on subjects that they like, you can help them find productive activities that fit with their interests. If your Scorpio wants to learn more about animals, you could plan a trip to the animal shelter or the zoo, or if they have an obsession with dinosaurs or ancient artifacts, you could take them to a natural history museum.

If You're an Air Sign...

If you are a Gemini, Libra, or Aquarius parent to a Scorpio, you and your child may have to put in some effort to get on the same page, but there is a lot to learn from one another. You may approach life with logic, analyzing everything super closely, while your Scorpio follows what their emotions are telling them. However, they may keep a lot of their feelings buried, and they like their privacy. You are naturally good at communicating, so you may be able to urge your child to speak about whatever is bothering them. You may also want to get them involved in social activities from time to time, and you could help them to be more comfortable at birthday parties or after-school meetups with their peers.

Your Scorpio child also likes to deeply understand things and get to the root of why a person or situation is the way it is. They may have a lot of questions to ask, so you may enjoy having in-depth conversations with your child, helping them to figure out answers to whatever interests them. Your Scorpio will look up to you, because of how knowledgeable you are.

If You're a Water Sign...

If you are a Cancer, Scorpio, or Pisces parent to a Scorpio, you and your child probably have similar personalities. You may both be pretty in tune with your emotions, but sometimes your feelings can be overwhelming. You may have always thought of yourself as the sensitive one, but your Scorpio child feels everything just as deeply, even if they don't readily show you this side of themselves. You're very intuitive though, so you may naturally be able to sense when your child is having an off day or is upset. In addition, you and your Scorpio may both be pretty introverted, so you may need to make an effort to get out of the house sometimes and go on walks together or plan family trips. Since you are both water signs, going to the beach or a nearby lake could be calming.

You may also want to help your Scorpio explore their creative side by buying arts and crafts or signing them up for singing or musical lessons. Even if you may like going with the flow, your child will crave some sort of structure, so they will enjoy regular weekday activities. One area you may have to work on though is letting your child explore their interests without hovering over them. Your first instinct is to nurture and take care of them but try to let your Scorpio do their own thing now and then.

WHY TAKING CARE OF YOURSELF AS A PARENT MATTERS

What Is Self-Care?

Self-care is any action that you do to improve your health and well-being. It can include physical activities like *eating well, exercising, sleeping enough, and taking care of your hygiene. It can also include psychological activities like managing stress, setting boundaries,* expressing your feelings, and seeking help when needed. Self-care also includes emotional practices such as mindfulness, forgiving others, compassion, and thankfulness. Additionally, don't overlook spiritual practices like praying, meditation, and spending time in nature.

Self-care is not conceitful or frivolous. It's not about running away from your duties or ignoring your kids. It's about looking after yourself so that you may better look after other people. It's about getting enough liquid into your cup so you have something to spill.

How Self-Care Benefits You and Your Children

Self-care has many benefits for both you and your children. Here are some of them:

Taking care of yourself can help you feel more **positive, focused, and energized.** You can be more present and focused with your kids when you take the time to relax and rejuvenate.

You can manage stress by taking care of yourself. Being a parent can be difficult at times, and if you don't handle it effectively, it can negatively impact your relationships, mood, and health. You can lower your stress hormones, unwind physically, and clear your head by taking care of yourself.

Self-care can help you **prevent burnout**. Burnout is a state of physical, emotional, and mental exhaustion caused by chronic stress. It can lead to depression, anxiety, irritability, and low self-esteem. Self-care can help you avoid burnout by balancing your demands with your resources.

You may teach your kids good behaviors by practicing self-care. Kids pick up knowledge by watching the attitudes and actions of their parents. They will learn to take care of themselves if they witness you doing so. They will also learn to respect both their own and your demands and boundaries.

HOW TO REDUCE STRESS AS A PARENT

The whole family is strained by parenting stress, which weakens well-being, ruins relationships, and saps patience. How can we address this?

Here are some suggestions inspired by the latest research.

1. **Need social support? Reach out — even if it's just a phone call to a parenting helpline.**
This should surprise no one, but it needs to be said: **Parenting is a lot easier when you've got friends, family, or neighbors on your side.**

Indeed, as I've explained elsewhere, human parents have always needed helpers. People who offer childcare help, emotional support, and economic aid.

So if you find yourself feeling isolated and overwhelmed, know that it isn't a personal failing. You aren't supposed to be isolated. You aren't supposed to be overwhelmed. You are supposed to be part of a **supportive social network**.

Heck, even monkey parents can count on the support of their friends and allies.
But what can you do if you don't live near friends and relatives? Or lack people in your life who can provide you with the support you need?

There are many options: *Local parenting cooperatives. Online parenting communities and support groups. Trained therapists.*

Enrolling in a parenting class can be helpful too. Studies indicate that parenting classes can reduce your feelings of anger, guilt, and stress — particularly if your child has difficult behavior problems

Not sure where to find these resources? Try your family physician, as well as parenting helplines.

2. Ration your exposure to negative thoughts and negative media.

It's natural to look for patterns. If a child is temperamental, defiant, or high-strung, you may be persuaded that his next move will be a negative one. It's also natural to pay more attention to potential threats when you're feeling upset, angry, or alarmed.

Stress makes people zero in on the bad stuff.

But your beliefs and biases can become self-fulfilling prophecies. If you assume the worst, you're liable to provoke negative behavior from other people. You're also more likely to experience a downward spiral of deteriorating mood.

People often become more aware of disturbing sights, menacing phrases, and unfavorable comments after only a brief exposure to emotionally charged negative content.

They worry about the future or relive unpleasant experiences.

Such ideas trigger the brain's stress circuits, intensifying feelings of dread and worry. An irate remark, an unpleasant reminder, or a painful story could be the only trigger needed to start the process.

In some crises, this could be useful. When a lion is pursuing you, it's wise to get into threat mode. But you're in much worse shape in other situations. Receiving too much negative or scary information raises more than just your stress levels at once. It may also impair your capacity for positive thought and problem-solving.

And that hurts everyone — you, your family, your neighbors, and your coworkers.

This suggests a basic strategy for protecting yourself: **Avoid unnecessary exposure to signals that drag you down.** Switch off disturbing media; steer clear of hostile, rude, or judgmental people; consider taking a new route to work if it means avoiding noise, pollution, hassles, hostility, and other stressors.

3. Focus on the good: Acts of warmth, kindness, and caring.

We've seen how unfavorable messages can completely destabilize your stress response. Conversely, it's also true that we can download uplifting information into our brains to create pleasant emotions.

Thus, make an effort to engage in happy social situations, notice your child's smiles, and take advantage of each chance to physically offer your youngster affection. Pet the family dog, read inspirational stories, tell jokes, and think back on pleasant times.

All of these things have been shown to nudge brain chemistry away from stress and towards a state of calm and well-being.

Bearing witness to positive social messages may help fill the void left by absent friends and family.

Focusing acts of kindness and social support — even those we see performed by strangers in a photograph — can deactivate the stress response.

4. **Use insights from psychology to help your future self.**

Sometimes we think we're good at predicting these things, but when researchers compare our predictions to real outcomes, it's clear that we underestimate our future needs.

So analyze what goes wrong, and make a deliberate, conscious effort to help out your future self. Are the kids going to fight over that particular game? Then don't bring it with you. Is that difficult relative going to stress you out? Decide ahead of time what you will do about it. Will the noise make you crazy? Bring earplugs.

5. **Budget for more time to get things done.**

Time pressure is a universal stressor, but it hits some parents particularly hard.

Though you may believe that altering your schedule is beyond your means, think about: One of the more widely-repeated results in psychology is that people tend to underestimate the amount of time it takes to complete tasks, which can lead to toxic stress.

Furthermore, young children require more time to learn, to check their urges, and to react than adults.

So it's likely that many families would benefit from adjusted expectations. If running late is driving you crazy, start earlier, and don't assume your little slow-poke is trying to thwart you.

6. **When bad things happen, re-appraise the situation.**

Sometimes it doesn't matter how many good thoughts you think: **Stressful things happen.** But even then, there is a lot you can do to cope.

Studies show that people handle stress better when they reconsider the situation from a new angle.

7. **Is your sense of empathy stressing you out? Get in touch with the more clear-headed, problem-solving side of your empathic nature.**

When your kid is miserable, you feel their pain, and that can be a good thing: It may motivate you to help. But the trouble with this sort of empathy — what psychologists call "affective empathy" — is that it's a double-edged sword.

"Feeling the pain" might inspire you to be compassionate, but it might also push you to the edge.

This explains why parents who identify as highly empathic may respond excessively to their children's problems. They become overly anxious, which can make them *irritable, aggressive, or domineering.*

In research where mothers played a parenting simulation game, mothers who exhibited high levels of affective empathy experienced higher cortisol spikes when faced with making decisions regarding their unhappy, anxious children.

They also experienced heightened activity in parts of the hypothalamus and amygdala, regions of the brain linked with anxiety and stress.

So affective empathy causes stress, and that can undermine parenting. But that doesn't mean we'd be better off as sociopaths.

There is another type of empathy, called **cognitive empathy**, that involves taking another person's perspective and imagining what would make him feel better. It's more cerebral and reflective, and it doesn't rev up the stress response system.

Mothers who prioritized cognitive empathy exhibited the least amount of stress reactivity and made more correct decisions.

This implies that when we try to observe our children's issues more objectively and remove ourselves from their difficulties, we shouldn't feel bad about it. To be sensitive, we don't have to put up with their negative attitudes. On the other hand, by exercising a little detachment, we might be able to better assist children.

8. **Look for practical sleep solutions, but don't stress about lost hours and fatigue.**

You want to address sleep issues as soon as you can since inadequate sleep makes living challenging. However, there will always be some disturbances, particularly if you have young children. How ought one to proceed?

It ought to be obvious by now what not to do. It won't help to hold grudges, dwell on the past, or fret about not being able to function the next day.

Negative thoughts trigger your brain's stress circuits, as we've already shown, so worrying will make it even more difficult to nod off when you do get a chance.

Besides, your kids are likely to sense your emotions, and that will make it harder for them to sleep.

So don't give up on finding practical solutions to family sleep problems.

But don't brood about it either.

According to research, people adjust more readily when they give up worrying about the future, stop calculating their hours, stop making emotional judgments about how exhausted they are, and instead concentrate on accepting the situation and finding the positive aspects of it. Putting this new mindset into practice is a good way to alleviate insomnia.

9. **Help children cope with their stresses, and teach siblings how to work out their differences**

Kids aren't born with an instinct for emotional self-regulation. They have to develop it, and they take their cues from **us**. Research suggests that parents can have a crucial impact on the way kids handle stress, especially if kids have "**difficult**" or high-strung temperaments.

It starts with the wise decisions we can make for our newborns and lasts through childhood: Preschoolers can benefit from a calm, positive, constructive conversation about emotions as they grow in social skills, empathy, and self-control.

Children must also learn how to get along with their siblings, and taking the initiative pays off.

A colleague of mine (Dr. Nella Jayden) showed mothers how to teach their young children conflict resolution skills — like how to see things from your sibling's perspective, how to negotiate, and how to calm yourself down when you're feeling angry or distressed — She didn't just see a reduction in sibling aggression. She also observed improvements in the ways that mothers handled their own emotions.

10. Make time for inspiration

Some things make us happy because they offer us immediate, selfish pleasure; other things offer a more lasting, meaningful type of happiness.

Is it all the same when it comes to stress relief? Research suggests otherwise. Meaningful happiness seems to block toxic stress from reprogramming our

DNA and increasing our risk of stress-related disease. By contrast, self-gratifying happiness does not.

Therefore, if your hectic schedule has forced you to give up on happiness, think about:

Your sense of purpose or meaning is not a self-serving indulgence that has to be given up for family responsibilities, like a box of chocolates.

A vital technique for maintaining your health and shielding your family from stress is engaging in meaningful experiences. By re-establishing connections with the things, people, and objectives that are important to you, you can increase the amount of meaningful happiness in your life.

11. **Tap into the stress-busting effects of nature.**

As I explain elsewhere, spending time outdoors, in a natural environment, can reduce tension, anger, confusion, and depression. It can also lower cortisol levels.

Can't get away? Experiments suggest that merely looking at nature scenes can improve your mood and help you recover from stress. **health.**

12. **Get out and exercise — but make it fun**.

The body is shielded against the negative consequences of both physical and mental stress by aerobic exercise. In addition, it might improve your mood, reduce anxiety, and encourage the development of new brain cells.

Experiments, however, seem to indicate that these outcomes rely on free will. Exercise that is compelled or involuntary might raise stress levels.

VOICES OF EXPERIENCE: LANCE'S INQUIRIES INTO PARENTAL SELF-CARE PRACTICES

Parenting is hard. It's a full-time job and many parents find themselves prioritizing their family's well-being before their own.

When we can meet our own mental and physical needs, it not only benefits our well-being but our children as well.

But how do you make it happen? I asked three mental health experts, who are also parents, how they do it.

Hear from **Dr. Claire Damour, Anna Gupta, and Dr. Donna Talib** on how they prioritize self-care, the activities they practice, and the benefits they have witnessed for their families.

Claire: "Very often, I think parents assume that taking time for themselves means that they are taking time away from their children. But this isn't true. When we care for ourselves, we are better able to care for our children. And caring for ourselves underscores for our children the importance of self-care while also showing them how it's done."

Donna: "Self-care is something you can do for a short while at a time; it's similar to developing a habit that requires some work but is always there. However, self-care can also include asking for assistance when you need it from family, friends, coworkers, therapists, or other mental health professionals."

Anna: "Making time for self-care is usually a good idea if you haven't already. It's a significant step toward resilience and self-compassion. As you embark on your road of self-care, remember to be kind to both yourself and other people. It takes time and is an investment in our mental health to transform little routines into rituals."

How do you personally practice self-care?

Anna: I refer to the time I set aside for myself as my **"Pause Rituals"**—a deliberate break during the day that is followed by rituals that help me feel better physically, mentally, and socially. About ten years ago, while I was experiencing burnout, I coined this phrase. When practicing these self-soothing techniques, it's important to concentrate on just one thing and schedule it into your schedule, even if it just takes ten minutes during a hectic day. Every day at a set time, I go for a solitary walk, spend time reading non-fiction, meditate and listen to calming noises in the morning, and take a 15-minute power nap. Scheduling leisure and playtime is also something that I see as self-care. As a therapist and a parent, my pause rituals have served as a sacred space for me.

Donna: "As I get older, I find myself returning to these basic life ingredients for my well-being: moving my body, breathing, getting enough sleep, putting my phone down, and eating more fruits and vegetables. When I feel my mental health is strong, I realize I am doing these things. Whenever I start to struggle with my mental health, I look to do more of these things. Of course, when I have the time, I like to add in stretching, yoga and just talking to my parents, other family members, and friends. Just a few minutes of hearing their voices and sharing my thoughts settle me.

Claire: "I safeguard my capacity to fall asleep fast and stay asleep through the night because, as a psychologist, I know that sleep is the glue that keeps people together. In the nights, I attempt to slow things down to help me fall asleep faster. Like a lot of other people, I've discovered that it's nearly hard for me to go to sleep soon after engaging in any sort of intensely stimulating activity. I try to get lots of fresh air and frequent exercise to help me sleep better at night. These two things help me stay asleep."

Donna: "As I rush around taking care of my two young children, I feel as though I never have enough time for self-care and completing the tasks of my day job. I always feel on duty. I prioritize self-care by baking it into my routines with my children and at work.
When I brush my teeth, I practice mindfulness, while I cook, I talk to my family or friends, during bedtime with the children, I hold some yoga poses. I breathe deeply often at work in between meetings and try to put my phone away when the day is done, but this is hard for me."

Claire: "Making the most of my alone time, when it's quiet, has been one parenting tip that has helped. I used to enjoy completing ordinary chores in silence, especially when my mind was racing. In the past, I would listen to music or talk to friends on the phone while folding laundry or preparing dinner. I discovered that I can think through issues that are bothering me and come up with original answers to the problems I'm having. When I take advantage of opportunities to let my thoughts go wherever they need to go, my thinking always feels clearer."

Anna: I've grown to believe that self-care is a daily endeavor. On those days I don't get time to build self-care, I feel overwhelmed, wired, and anxious. My family and I have chosen to openly talk about the big feelings we may be experiencing, like when we feel overwhelmed and overburdened. Over the years all of us, including my husband and daughter, have talked to each other about self-care, and taking some time for ourselves, allows us to feel more centered and operate from a place of calm.

How has your family benefitted from your self-care?

If I do not prioritize my mental health and well-being, I do not show up with my best foot forward as a parent.

Claire: When I'm well-rested and my mind is clear, I am much more patient with my children and a lot more fun to be around. After a good night's sleep, I have the energy to play, host a "kitchen dance party," or come up with other ways to enjoy my daughters' company. And when I'm not distracted by my concerns, I am much better able to focus on my girls and what they need from me.

Anna: Our practices of self-care have helped deepen my family's resilience. Self-care brings about a sense of calm and this calm can be also contagious, which helps us in tough moments. Self-care has helped us respect each other's space and unique needs and at the same time, built space for compassion and empathy towards each other.

Donna: Some of my proudest moments in parenting are when I catch my young children deep breathing to find their calm when they have hard feelings – something they have watched me model in front of them often. I love it when they ask me to do some bedtime yoga or when they just start doing it themselves. I have learned that if I do not prioritize my mental health and well-being, I do not show up with my best foot forward as a parent.

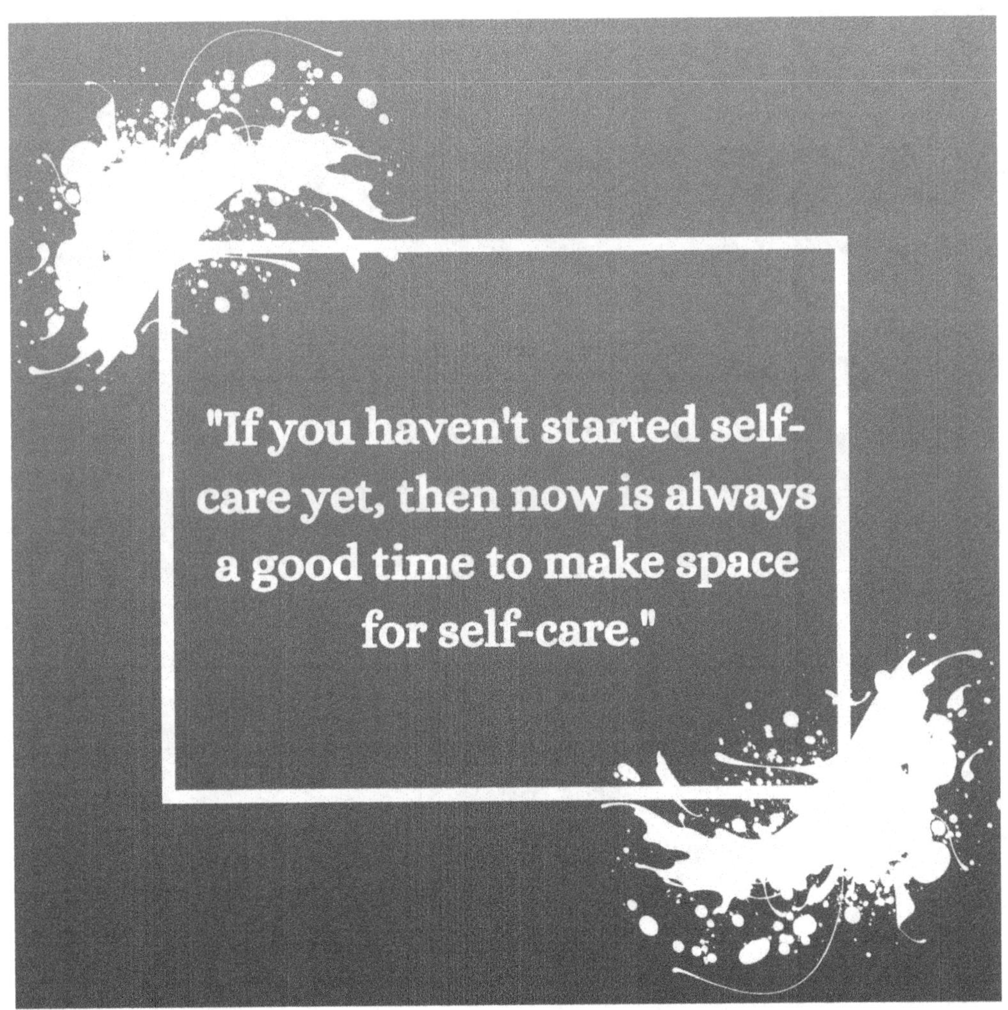

9 798393 470920